FORGET THEM, FIND YOU

By Joaquin Mann

FORGET THEM, FIND YOU

Written By
Joaquin Mann

Fullcover Design By
Sun Child Wind Spirit

Edited By
Mylia Tiye Mal Jaza

FORGET THEM, FIND YOU

Author Contact
Joaquin Mann
Facebook.com/JoaquinMann
writersconsortium@bepublished.biz

Self-Publishing Associate
BePublished.Org - Chicago
Dr. Mary M. Jefferson
(972) 880-8316
P.O. Box 8324
Jackson, MS 39284
www.bepublished.org
publisher@bepublished.org
First Edition.
Printed In the USA.
Recycled Paper Encouraged.

THE WRITERS CONSORTIUM
www.WritersConsortium.us

TABLE OF CONTENT

FORGET
THEM,
FIND
YOU

Introduction

There comes a time in every adult's life when they must choose between the endless cycle of pleasing others and the revolutionary act of choosing themselves. That time is now.

For too long, we've been conditioned to believe that our worth is tied to how much we give, how well we fit into societal expectations, and how successfully we cater to other people's needs. Whether it's family, friends, coworkers, romantic partners, or entire institutions — too many of us have sacrificed our peace, energy, and even sanity for people who wouldn't lift a finger for us. It's time to stop the madness.

This book is a call to action. It's about learning how to invest in yourself, not for the sake of selfishness, but for the sake of true self-discovery and fulfillment. You don't need anyone else to complete you. You don't need approval to be worthy. And you don't need to stay in toxic cycles that drain you. It's time to stop chasing people, stop auditioning for roles you never signed up for, and start building the life you deserve — on your terms, with your Source as your only validation.

As I often state to those I care about during conversations around the this topic:

Saying "fuck them" is not enough and still puts work in your hands! At the end of even your most celebrated day, you are the only one with you all 24 hours of every day and no one else should take priority over you when it comes to your joy — not even your spouse and children. Stop rolling over and playing dead! Stop eating out of your own trash can! The best thing you can do is spend time with you, and live your life being the best you.

It's time out for people-pleasing and bootlicking! Nobody is less than or better than you, and neither are you in comparison to them. You don't have to beg or prove to be a part of your family or community. The moment someone, in your quest for joy or fulfillment, is requiring you to jump through hoops on a unicycle while eating fire and churning a quart of homemade pistachio lemon custard, release yourself from that and them. Straight up let them go and fuck themselves! You have better things to do with your time, energy, love, and life! Forget about them, and invest all that extra into you and those who keep you sustained!

You have no reason to keep working with people who don't want to work with you! It's time to stop crying, staying awake all night, and lingering in that depression these monsters pushed you in. I'm telling you what I had to tell myself when I was in that pit.

Now, I've gotten out and have filled it with concrete!

You can do the same. Take back control of your experiences, emotions and effervescence! After all, if you're willing to not fuck around with them, you will have more time and resources available so you can use that to fortify you. That's the only way you can go from a human doing to actually living as a human being – able to truly walk in your appointed, divine purpose.

Chapter 1
Breaking Free from the Chains of People-Pleasing

People-pleasing is a disease that keeps you shackled to other people's expectations while starving your own soul. Many of us have spent years being the "yes man" or the "reliable one" at the expense of our own happiness. But ask yourself: what has that truly gotten you?

If you find yourself exhausted, overlooked, and constantly resentful, it's time to break free.

1. **Stop Saying Yes to Everything** – If it doesn't serve your peace, goals, or spirit, the answer is NO.

2. **Detach from Validation** – Your worth is not determined by how much others approve of you.

3. **Practice Self-Respect** – If you don't respect your time and boundaries, no one else will.

4. **Reclaim Your Schedule** – Take back the hours wasted catering to ungrateful people and invest them in YOU.

5. **Rebuild Your Identity** – Define who you are outside of what you do for others.

People-pleasing is a disease that you can heal from, freeing yourself from the anxiety that comes with trying to meet other people's expectations while yours remain in queue hoping for satisfaction. If what you need is time for you, take that time. Commit to nothing at the expense of your own happiness. Face this habit worth breaking.

The Story of Lisa: A Life of Yeses and No Self

Lisa was the person everyone depended on. She was the one who stayed late at work to cover for coworkers, the friend who always said "yes" to last-minute requests, and the daughter who never wanted to disappoint her family. For years, she thought saying yes made her valuable. She thought that by being reliable, she would earn love, appreciation, and security.

But all it earned her was exhaustion. She was always tired, overlooked for promotions because she never demanded recognition, and left out of social plans because her so-called friends only called her when they needed a favor. She felt invisible.

One night, Lisa broke down. She was lying in bed, staring at the ceiling, overwhelmed by resentment. She realized she had spent so much of her life trying to make others happy that she had no idea what made her happy. That was the night she decided to change.

The Disease of "Yes"

People-pleasing is an addiction — one that convinces you that your worth is tied to how much you do for others. It conditions you to believe that if you say "no," you are selfish, unworthy, or unlovable. But this is a lie.

The truth is:

- The more you say "yes" to others, the more you say "no" to yourself.

- Being overextended does not make you indispensable; it makes you a doormat.

- People who truly care about you won't leave just because you set boundaries.

- You are not responsible for making everyone happy.

1. **Stop Saying Yes to Everything** – If it doesn't serve your peace, goals, or spirit, the answer is NO.

2. **Detach from Validation** – Your worth is not determined by how much others approve of you.

3. **Practice Self-Respect** – If you don't respect your time and boundaries, no one else will.

4. **Reclaim Your Schedule** – Take back the hours wasted catering to ungrateful people and invest them in YOU.

5. **Rebuild Your Identity** – Define who you are outside of what you do for others.

Lisa started small. She stopped picking up calls from people who only called her for favors. She declined extra work that wasn't hers. And she started investing in herself — reading, meditating, and finding out what she wanted for a change.

It was hard at first. People pushed back. Some friends drifted away. But those who truly cared about her stayed, and new, healthier relationships formed in their place. Lisa finally started to breathe.

You Have Permission to Choose You

If you are exhausted, resentful, and lost in the expectations of others, it's time to make a choice.

Choose yourself.

You don't owe anyone endless access to your time, energy, or peace. You are not selfish for putting yourself first. You are simply reclaiming the life that was always meant to be yours.

Chapter 2
Cutting Off Fake Friends & Shady Coworkers

Not everyone in your circle is in your corner. Some "friends" only stick around because of what they can get from you. Some coworkers will smile in your face while plotting behind your back. Stop ignoring the red flags!

How to Spot and Handle Them:

- **The Fake Friend:** Always needs a favor, never reciprocates. Cut them off.

- **The Office Snake:** Smiles at you while taking credit for your work. Keep receipts and play smart.

- **The Emotional Leech:** Dumps their problems on you but disappears when you need support. Reclaim your energy.

- **The Backstabber:** Spreads rumors and betrays trust. Distance yourself immediately.

The Story of Gion: Betrayed by His Own Circle

Gion had always been a team player. At work, he took on extra tasks to help his coworkers. Among his friends, he was the reliable one — the one people called when they needed help moving, covering a shift, or even borrowing money. He believed that by being generous and supportive, his relationships would thrive.

But Gion started noticing a pattern. His coworkers would take credit for his ideas in meetings, yet never acknowledge his contributions. His so-called friends only reached out when they needed something but were nowhere to be found when he needed support. One day, after working late to help a coworker meet a deadline, he found out that same coworker had gotten a promotion — using Gion's work as their own.

The realization hit him hard: he was being used.

Recognizing the Signs of Fake Friends and Shady Coworkers

- **One-Sided Relationships** – If you're always the one giving and rarely receiving, you're not in a real friendship — you're in a transactional relationship.

- **Disrespect and Undermining** – If people dismiss your ideas, steal credit, or mock you behind your back, they are not your allies.

- **Lack of Support** – Friends and coworkers should celebrate your wins, not just show up when they need something.

Practical Steps to Breaking Free

1. **Set Boundaries** – Stop being overly available. If they only call for

favors, let them handle their own issues.

2. **Observe and Redirect** – Take note of how people treat you when you have nothing to offer. If they disappear, let them go.

3. **Speak Up** – Call out workplace injustices. If your work is stolen, document it and bring it to the right people.

4. **Surround Yourself with Genuine People** – Invest in those who reciprocate kindness and respect.

5. **Walk Away** – If you're constantly drained by certain people, cut them off and focus on those who uplift you.

Gion stopped engaging with those who used him. He built new friendships based on mutual respect and found a new job where his contributions were valued. The weight lifted from his shoulders, and for the first time in years, he felt free.

Do you see it yet? Have you realized it already? Are you able to relate? If so, I'm glad that we agree. You do deserve better, much better, than what you have received from others you've supported and cared for in the past.

You are not obligated to keep fake friends or endure toxic workplaces. Recognize your worth and walk away from people who drain you. Your time, energy, and peace are too valuable to be wasted on those who don't respect you.

Chapter 3
Escaping Religious/Business Cults

Too many organizations — whether religious or business-related — prey on people's need for belonging and purpose. They know that humans are wired for connection, and they exploit this need to their own advantage. The worst of them operate like cults — manipulating emotions, controlling information, and draining people of their time, money, and autonomy.

If you've ever felt trapped in an environment that demanded more from you than it gave, you're not alone. The key is learning to recognize the red flags before they pull you deeper into their web.

The Story of Javier:
Trapped in a Cycle of Spiritual Manipulation

Javier grew up in a tight-knit religious community that dictated every aspect of his life. From a young age, he was taught that questioning authority was a sign of weakness and lack of faith. Leaders within the group spoke in absolutes — if you followed their rules, you were blessed. If you doubted or disobeyed, you risked spiritual ruin.

As Javier got older, he started noticing inconsistencies. The same leaders who preached humility and sacrifice drove luxury cars and lived in mansions, funded by the hard-earned donations of struggling families. His friend Mateo was shunned for asking too many questions. Women in the group were pressured to marry young, and members who wanted to leave were told they would be cursed if they did. Still, Javier ignored his gut instincts because he feared losing his community.

Then came the financial demand. One day, a leader pulled Javier aside and told him that to prove his faith, he needed to make a "sacrificial offering." The amount? Three months' worth of salary. Javier hesitated — he barely made enough to cover his bills. But the leader reminded him of the dangers of disobedience. "Do you trust God or not?" he asked.

That night, Javier lay awake, tormented. He had seen families in the congregation suffer financially while the leadership lived comfortably. He had witnessed how fear kept everyone in line. And he realized, for the first time, that he was not part of a supportive faith community — he was part of a system designed to control him.

Recognizing the Warning Signs

Not all organizations that prey on people operate as obviously as the one Javier was trapped in. Some come disguised as self-improvement groups, exclusive business circles, or "once-in-a-lifetime" opportunities. But the tactics remain the same:

- **Demands for Blind Loyalty Over Critical Thinking** – Healthy organizations encourage growth and questions. Cult-like ones demand obedience and punish doubt.

- **Using Guilt and Fear to Control You** – If you're constantly made to feel that leaving or saying "no" will lead to disaster, you're being manipulated.

- **Expecting You to Give Endlessly While Receiving Nothing in Return** – Whether it's money, time, or effort, if an organization always takes but never gives, it's exploiting you.

- **Shunning or Punishing Those Who Question Authority** – If those who leave are cut off, ridiculed, or threatened, that's a red flag.

How Cults Exploit Trust and Vulnerability

1. **Spiritual Manipulation** – They twist religious or philosophical beliefs to keep you dependent. "If you leave, you're betraying God." "If you don't contribute, you're spiritually weak."

2. **Emotional Puppeteering** – They play on your fears and desires. "You'll never find another community like this." "We are your true family."

3. **Common Con Games Targeting Low-Income Families** – Many cult-like businesses and religious groups target the financially vulnerable, promising prosperity in exchange for loyalty and financial sacrifices.

- o **Pyramid Schemes Disguised as "Entrepreneurship"** – They tell you that if you just invest more money, you'll eventually see returns. You won't.

- o **Churches That Demand "Faith Seed" Donations** – You're told to give beyond your means with the promise that God will bless you tenfold. But the only people getting richer are the ones collecting the money.

- o **Fake Mentorship Programs** – These organizations promise to change your life, but only if you keep paying for courses, events, and membership fees that lead nowhere.

How to Get Out

Breaking free is not easy, but it is possible. Here's how:

1. **Trust Your Gut** – If something feels off, it probably is. Your intuition is your first line of defense.

2. **Seek Knowledge** – Research the organization. Find out if others have left and why. Look for patterns of control and exploitation.

3. **Prioritize Freedom Over Fear** – No organization should own your soul. True belonging doesn't require blind obedience.

4. **Create a Support System** – Connect with people who think independently. Finding a new circle can make leaving easier.

5. **Plan Your Exit** – If you're financially or emotionally entangled, plan a way out safely. Seek professional help if necessary.

Javier's Escape

Javier didn't leave overnight. He started by secretly researching others who had left his faith group. He read books on spiritual abuse and manipulation. He reached out to Mateo, who had been ostracized, and listened to his story. Slowly, Javier realized that he had been living in fear, not faith.

One Sunday, he made his choice. He walked out of service and never returned. The backlash was immediate — leaders accused him of "losing his way." Old friends stopped talking to him. But Javier also found freedom. He rebuilt his life, surrounded himself with people who encouraged independent thought, and found peace knowing that his spirituality was his own, not something dictated by others.

Final Thoughts

If you're trapped in a religious or business cult, know this: You are not weak for wanting to leave. You are strong for questioning. No group, no leader, and no organization has the right to control your mind, heart, or finances. True purpose and fulfillment come from within — not from obedience to manipulative systems.

It's time to take your power back. Walk away. Build your own path. And never let fear be the thing that keeps you from finding yourself.

Chapter 4
Flaky Relationships
& Selfish Lovers

Family and romantic relationships can be some of the most draining experiences when the people involved are self-serving. You are not obligated to maintain relationships with people who only take and never give.

The Story of Tatelyn:
Feeling Like A Tool, Unrequited Love

Tatelyn had always been the reliable one in her family. If someone needed a ride to the airport at the last minute, Tatelyn was there. If a cousin forgot to bring a dish to

Thanksgiving, Tatelyn would whip something up. If her sister was having a meltdown over a breakup, Tatelyn would drop everything to listen and provide support. But when Tatelyn found herself struggling, overwhelmed with work and personal stress, she realized something disturbing — no one showed up for her the way she showed up for them.

One particular moment stood out. She had been sick with the flu for days, barely able to get out of bed. She had sent a simple text to her brother, asking if he could pick up some groceries for her. His response? "Sorry, I'm really busy today, maybe tomorrow." Tomorrow came and went, and she never heard from him again. Meanwhile, her phone buzzed with messages from family members asking for small favors, assuming she was still the ever-reliable Tatelyn. It was in that moment, exhausted and disappointed, that she understood — her relationships were not balanced.

This realization led Tatelyn down a difficult but necessary path: she needed to set boundaries and demand reciprocity, or she would have to walk away. And as painful as it was, she eventually learned that walking away from selfish people didn't mean she was losing family or love — it meant she was making room for healthier connections.

Set Clear Boundaries

Setting boundaries is the first step to reclaiming your time and emotional energy. If you are always the giver, it's time to start limiting how much you give to those who don't reciprocate.

- **Learn to say no.** You are not obligated to accommodate every request, especially when it's clear that the same effort isn't being returned. Tatelyn began practicing this by declining last-minute requests unless it was truly an emergency.

- **Limit access to your time and energy.** If a family member or partner only reaches out when they need something, begin to disengage. You can still be cordial, but you don't have to be endlessly available.

- **Express your expectations.** Sometimes, people genuinely don't realize they're taking advantage. A simple, direct conversation can sometimes shift the dynamic. Tatelyn had to tell her family that she expected the same support she gave them — otherwise, she would stop overextending herself.

Demand Reciprocity

Healthy relationships are based on give and take. If you find yourself constantly giving without receiving, it's time to make a change.

- **Pay attention to patterns.** One-off instances of selfishness can be forgiven, but if someone consistently disregards your needs, they are showing you who they are.

- **Speak up.** Let people know when you feel unappreciated. You don't have to be confrontational, but you do need to be direct. "I've noticed I always make time for you when you need help, but when I ask for something, you're unavailable. That doesn't feel fair."

- **Stop enabling one-sided relationships.** If someone continues to take without giving, stop giving. Tatelyn learned that pulling back forced her family to either step up or reveal that they were never willing to in the first place.

Leave When Needed

Not every relationship is worth saving. If someone refuses to respect your boundaries or show you basic consideration, it's okay to walk away.

- **Assess the value of the relationship.** Is this person adding to your life, or are they draining you? Some family bonds or romantic connections exist only because of obligation, not genuine love.

- **Let go of guilt.** You are not a bad person for prioritizing your well-being. Cutting ties with toxic relatives or an inconsiderate partner is an act of self-care.

- **Ease out gradually if needed.** If cutting someone off entirely is too difficult, start with creating distance. Reduce communication and stop offering your time and energy so freely.

Build a New Support Network

Family is not always blood. If your relatives or partner are selfish and unreliable, seek out people who truly care about you.

- **Find your chosen family.** Friends, mentors, and even kind colleagues can become the supportive network you need.

- **Invest in reciprocal relationships.** Give your energy to those who show up for you, not just those who expect you to show up for them.

- **Create a community.** Join groups, clubs, or volunteer organizations where you can meet like-minded, caring individuals.

Tatelyn's story is not unique. Many people find themselves trapped in one-sided relationships, feeling drained and unappreciated. But the good news is that you have the power to change it. You are not obligated to maintain relationships that leave you exhausted. Whether you choose to set boundaries, demand better treatment, or walk away entirely, the goal is the same — prioritizing your peace and surrounding yourself with those who truly value you.

Chapter 5
Political Uncertainty
& Systematic Oppression

Let's face it — society is built on systems designed to exploit. Whether it's government policies, corporate greed, or systemic discrimination, it's easy to feel powerless. But you are not.

The Landscape of Political Uncertainty and Systematic Oppression in America

America has always been a land of contradictions. While it prides itself on democracy and freedom, it has also been a country that systematically disenfranchises certain groups. From voter suppression tactics to economic policies that disproportionately affect marginalized communities, the very foundations of the political system are riddled with inequality.

The Current State of Political Uncertainty

Political uncertainty in America is at an all-time high. Partisan gridlock, misinformation campaigns, and the rise of authoritarian tendencies in political leaders have made the system feel more fragile than ever. The instability affects everything — public trust in institutions, economic growth, and social cohesion.

The erosion of democratic norms has been particularly troubling. Gerrymandering, voter suppression, and the influence of money in politics have turned democracy into an illusion for many. With courts packed with partisan judges and laws being passed to restrict voting rights, many Americans feel their voices are being silenced.

Systematic Oppression: A Deeply Embedded Issue

Systematic oppression in America is not just a relic of the past — it is alive and well. It exists in criminal justice, education, healthcare, and housing policies, affecting millions of lives every day. The school-toprison pipeline, discriminatory lending practices, and wage disparities all serve to maintain an economic and social hierarchy that benefits the privileged few.

One of the most glaring examples of systemic oppression is mass incarceration. America has the highest incarceration rate in the world, with Black and brown communities disproportionately affected. Laws designed to criminalize poverty, such as cash bail systems and excessive sentencing for minor offenses, keep marginalized populations trapped in a cycle of disenfranchisement.

Wesson's Story: A Fight for Dignity

Wesson never thought he'd be a political activist. He was just a kid from a small town, raised to believe that hard work would be enough. But by the time he hit 30, he realized that the system wasn't just flawed — it was designed to keep people like him struggling.

After graduating from college with a mountain of debt, Wesson found himself stuck in a cycle of underpaid jobs and increasing financial pressure. He watched as his community suffered from unfair housing policies, low wages, and over-policing. When a close friend was wrongfully arrested during a peaceful protest, Wesson snapped. Enough was enough.

He began attending community meetings, educating himself on policies affecting his town. He learned how politicians manipulated public narratives to justify injustice. He saw how corporations profited from cheap labor and government subsidies while communities suffered. Wesson realized that fighting back wasn't just about anger — it was about strategy.

How to Fight Back

1. Educate Yourself – Knowledge is power; ignorance is a weapon used against you.

Wesson started by reading everything he could. He researched the history of oppression, from redlining to mass incarceration. He attended lectures, watched documentaries, and talked to those who had been fighting for justice for years. He learned that one of the greatest tools of oppression is keeping people uninformed.

Practical Steps:

- Follow reputable journalists and publications.

- Learn about policies that impact you.

- Understand how the economy and government systems work.

- Teach others — knowledge should be shared, not hoarded.

2. Use Your Voice – Speak up, vote, organize.

Wesson once believed that voting didn't matter. That changed when he saw local elections directly impact housing laws in his neighborhood. He realized that people in power count on voter apathy.

He joined local organizations, helped register voters, and spoke at city council meetings. He encouraged others to use their voices, reminding them that silence only benefits the oppressors.

Practical Steps

- Vote in local, state, and national elections.

- Attend town hall meetings.

- Use social media to spread awareness.

- Join or start a grassroots organization.

3. Build Economic Strength – Financial independence gives you leverage.

Wesson understood that economic oppression was a major tool of control. He saw families trapped in cycles of poverty due to predatory lending, low wages, and lack of financial literacy. So he made a plan.

He took financial literacy courses, started a side hustle, and learned about investment opportunities. He helped his community by organizing free financial workshops. Economic strength wasn't just about making money — it was about breaking chains.

Practical Steps:

- Learn financial literacy (budgeting, investing, credit management).
- Support Black- and minority-owned businesses.
- Develop multiple income streams.
- Advocate for fair wages and worker protections.

4. Support Your Community – Invest in local businesses, mentor others, and create self-sustaining systems.

Wesson knew real change started within. He volunteered at local food drives, mentored young men, and helped create a neighborhood co-op. Systemic oppression thrives on division, so he made it his mission to strengthen the bonds within his community.

Practical Steps:

- Buy from local businesses instead of large corporations.

- Volunteer at community organizations.

- Mentor young people in your area.

- Build mutual aid networks to support those in need.

The Future: Breaking the Cycle of Oppression

The fight against systemic oppression and political uncertainty is not a short-term battle. It requires sustained effort, awareness, and activism. We must challenge the structures that keep oppression in place and create systems that uplift instead of exploit.

The role of technology and social media has been a game-changer in exposing injustices and mobilizing communities. However, misinformation and political manipulation remain real threats. It is up to each of us to remain vigilant, fact-check information, and engage in meaningful activism.

Leverage technology, spirituality, practicality, integrity and humanity! Find you today, and never look or go back to yesterday! The key to true freedom is investing in yourself — mind, body, and spirit. The moment you stop chasing behind people and start focusing on YOU, everything changes. You stop being an option and start being a priority — to yourself, first and foremost.

Find your purpose. Find your why. Find your joy. Find your cheese. Find your tribe. Find your YOU.

And for anyone who has a problem with that? Expend no energy their way. Forget them and let them go fuck themselves further. You'll be spending your time making sure YOU are well pleased.

Conclusion

The key to true freedom is investing in yourself — mind, body, and spirit. The moment you stop chasing behind people and start focusing on YOU, everything changes. You stop being an option and start being a priority — to yourself, first and foremost.

Finding Yourself: Step Into True Freedom

Finding yourself is not just about self-discovery; it is about self-commitment. It requires stepping back from the noise of the world and listening to your inner voice. It means shutting down the distractions, removing toxic people from your life, and allowing yourself to evolve into the person you were always meant to be.

Far too often, we allow the expectations of others to dictate our decisions. We prioritize the happiness of those around us while neglecting our own well-being. We compromise, adjust, and mold ourselves into versions that fit someone else's standards. But at what cost? Losing yourself to please others is the ultimate betrayal of your own existence.

The moment you decide to reclaim your power, everything shifts. You begin to move differently, think differently, and see the world from a fresh perspective. Your energy no longer leaks into empty pursuits or unreciprocated relationships. Instead, you channel it into your growth, your passion, and your dreams. You begin to thrive, not just survive.

The Power of Saying No

One of the most liberating things you will ever do is say "no." No to people who drain your energy. No to relationships that no longer serve you. No to outdated expectations. No to playing small to make others feel comfortable.

There is an author I personally know who wrote a book solely devoted to giving you ways to say "no" in a plethora of languages. That global "Book Of No" by Mylia Tiye Mal Jaza (who edited this book for me while her 52nd book, <u>Sex & Greed</u>, was being released in February) has plenty of new words that you may find easier to say – and fun to explain to those who ask what the word means.

As you tell them about the intentional work you had to perform to be able to reject people without allowing yourself to feel bad for not giving in to their desires that would have left you in a bad position had you given in, they'll likely appreciate the lesson and explain that you are not wrong for not going along with something you know doesn't work well for you.

Saying no is a radical act of self-love. It is a declaration that you will not betray yourself for the sake of fitting in or being liked. Those who truly value you will respect your boundaries. Those who don't? Let them go. Because the truth is, people who benefit from your lack of self-prioritization will always resist when you start setting boundaries.

Invest in Your Mind, Body, and Spirit

True freedom comes from investing in yourself. This means nurturing your mind with knowledge, wisdom, and self-awareness. Read books, explore new perspectives, challenge your beliefs, and keep growing.

Your body is your vessel. Treat it with care. Move it, nourish it, and rest when necessary. The more you respect your physical well-being, the more you will feel aligned and powerful.

And then, there is your spirit — the core of who you are. Feed it with solitude, creativity, meditation, nature, or anything that makes you feel whole. The stronger your spirit, the less dependent you become on external validation. You realize that happiness is an inside job.

This means that, just like you intentionally engaged others for their fulfillment, you have to be intentional about engaging yourself for your own fulfillment. Here's a quick list of 25 activities that I think you can easily take part in to satisfy your spiritual needs, boost self-esteem, and enhance emotional intelligence:

1. **Meditation** – Practice mindfulness or guided meditation to enhance self-awareness and inner peace.

2. **Journaling** – Write down thoughts, emotions, and reflections to understand yourself better.

3. **Reading Personal Growth Books** – Expand your mind with self-help and spiritual literature.

4. **Solo Travel** – Explore new places to gain perspective and confidence.

5. **Exercise/Yoga** – Engage in movement that nurtures both your body and mind.

6. **Spending Time in Nature** – Hike, walk, or sit in a park to reconnect with yourself.

7.   **Creative Expression** – Paint, draw, write poetry, or make music to channel emotions.

8.   **Volunteering** – Give back to the community to develop empathy and purpose.

9.   **Learning a New Skill** – Take a class or develop a hobby that challenges you.

10. **Cooking for Yourself** – Prepare a meal with intention and care as a form of self-love.

11. **Practicing Gratitude** – List things you're grateful for to foster a positive mindset.

12. **Listening to Uplifting Podcasts** – Absorb wisdom from thought leaders and motivators.

13. **Engaging in Deep Breathing Exercises** – Calm your nervous system and gain clarity.

14. **Decluttering and Organizing** – Create a peaceful living space that reflects your mindset.

15. **Setting and Achieving Small Goals** – Build confidence by completing meaningful tasks.

16. **Mirror Affirmations** – Speak positive affirmations to yourself daily.

17. **Dancing Freely** – Let loose and express yourself without judgment.

18. **Trying New Experiences** – Challenge yourself by stepping outside of your comfort zone.

19. **Taking Yourself on a Date** – Enjoy solo dining, a movie, or a day at a museum.

20. **Practicing Forgiveness** – Release resentment to free yourself emotionally.

21. **Connecting with Your Spirituality** – Engage in prayer, rituals, or other spiritual practices.

22. **Setting Healthy Boundaries** – Say no to things that drain your energy.

23. **Laughter Therapy** – Watch comedy, find joy, and allow yourself to laugh often.

24. **Self-Reflection Walks** – Walk with the intent of gaining insight into your life.

25. **Detoxing from Social Media –** Take breaks from external validation and focus inward.

Each of these activities promotes self-fulfillment and deepens emotional intelligence, helping you stay aligned with your journey. For people who have been conditioned to feel guilty for prioritizing themselves, picking two activities per week (or month) will be a good place to start slowly focusing on your own needs. Those who are already on their journey may find that they already perform many of these activities, you will still be able to find some new ideas for things to do to further build your new fortified identity.

Letting Go of Those Who Don't Serve You

Not everyone is meant to stay in your life. Some people are lessons, some are experiences, and some are simply placeholders. Holding onto people who don't respect, support, or uplift you is an act of self-sabotage.

You deserve relationships that reflect your worth. If someone doesn't appreciate you, let them go. If they have a problem with your growth, let them go. If they resent your happiness, let them go. Expending energy on those who drain you is a waste of your potential.

And for those who can't handle your transformation? Let them go fuck themselves further. Because your growth is not up for negotiation.

Finding Your Purpose and Joy

When you stop chasing people and start chasing your purpose, life shifts. Finding your purpose means aligning yourself with what fuels your soul. It's about doing things that bring you joy, fulfillment, and inner peace.

Joy is not something you find in others; it's something you cultivate within. It comes from waking up every day and choosing yourself. It comes from creating a life that excites you. It comes from breaking free of old patterns and stepping into the fullness of who you are.

Never Look Back

Once you have found yourself, don't look back. Don't second-guess your growth. Don't entertain old versions of yourself just to make others comfortable. Keep moving forward.

You owe it to yourself to live unapologetically. You owe it to yourself to love fiercely, dream boldly, and walk in your truth. Anyone who has a problem with that? That's their burden to carry — not yours.

So, go ahead and step into your betterment and spend more time alone. You need YOU. Your best days are ahead. You have no reason to look back, unless it is in the spirit of Sankofa (looking behind only for food to go forward). Wisdom is applying knowledge gained to date and the introspection practiced daily. Your advancement requires you to go within. It's okay to face yourself, adjust to your new life, and regain your footing. So, as for everyone else, forget THEM. Find YOU! And, never look back nor apologize for that.

FORGET
THEM,
FIND
YOU

The Art & Artist

Published with assistance from BePublished.org in March 2025, **FORGET THEM, FIND YOU** by Joaquin Mann is the author's tertiary work and first self-help project. This book, inclusive of action plans and recommended engagement activities, is a call to action for all people who feel they have not received the love and attention they deserve and need. Its goal is to help others learn how to invest in self, not for the sake of selfish exclusion of others, but for the sake of true self-discovery and basic human fulfillment.

"You don't need anyone else to complete you," the lifelong bachelor declares. "You don't need approval to be worthy. And you don't need to stay in toxic cycles that drain you. It's time to stop chasing people, stop auditioning for roles you never signed up for, and start building the life you deserve — on your terms, with your Source (whatever or whomever that may be) as your only validation."

"I wanted to do something unexpected, so while I was working on my science-fiction series, this popped up," the 51-year-old graphic designer and voice-over artist maintains. "Coming from behind the scenes to manifest my own vision for myself had to happen. I'm glad I finally prioritized my dreams and did for myself what I had been doing for others all these years. I hope you all like mine just as much too."

Available as an ebook worldwide, **<u>FORGET THEM, FIND YOU</u>** by Joaquin Mann may also be purchased from your favorite book retailers as a softback book and hardback book.

Facebook.com/JoaquinMann